SCHOLASTIC
News
Nonfiction Readers

Parrots and Other Birds

by
Mary Schulte

Children's Press®
A Division of Scholastic Inc.
New York Toronto London Auckland Sydney
Mexico City New Delhi Hong Kong
Danbury, Connecticut

These content vocabulary word builders
are for grades 1-2.

Consultant: Rodney B. Siegel
Research Scientist, The Institute for Bird Populations

Curriculum Specialist: Linda Bullock

Special thanks to Omaha's Henry Doorly Zoo

Photo Credits:

Photographs © 2005: Animals Animals/Alan G. Nelson: 1; Corbis Images: 4 top, 13 (Ashley Cooper), 4 bottom left, 7 (Bob Krist); Dembinsky Photo Assoc./Adam Jones: cover right inset; Dwight R. Kuhn Photography: 23 bottom left; Nature Picture Library Ltd.: cover background (Michael Durham), 5 bottom left, 15 (Dave Watts); Peter Arnold Inc.: back cover (Martin Harvey), cover center inset (Fritz Polking); Photo Researchers, NY: 23 bottom right (Nick Bergkessel Jr.), 2, 5 top left, 6, 9 (Stephen Dalton), 23 top right (William Ervin), 5 top right, 5 bottom right, 11 (William & Marcia Levy), 20, 21 (D. Roberts); photolibrary.com/Oxford Scientific: 23 top left; Stone/Getty Images: cover left inset (George Lepp), 4 bottom right, 10, 19 (David Tipling); The Image Works/Fritz Polking: 16, 17.

Book Design: Simonsays Design!

Library of Congress Cataloging-in-Publication Data

Schulte, Mary, 1958-
    Parrots and other birds / by Mary Schulte.
        p. cm. – (Scholastic news nonfiction readers)
    Includes bibliographical references and index.
    ISBN 0-516-24931-2 (lib. bdg.)
    1. Birds–Juvenile literature. 2. Parrots–Juvenile literature. I. Title. II. Series.
    QL676.2.S385 2005
    598–dc22

                                        2005003296

CONTENTS

WORD HUNT

Look for these words as you read. They will be **bold.**

clutch
(kluhch)

parrot
(**pa**-ruht)

penguins
(**peng**-gwinz)

4

feathers
(**feth**-urs)

ostrich
(**oss**-trich)

vertebrate
(**vur**-tuh-brate)

wing
(wing)

Birds! Birds!

Have you ever seen a **parrot**, an **ostrich**, or a **penguin**?

All of these animals are birds.

Birds have **feathers**.

feathers

This bird is a parrot. It has lots of colorful feathers.

Have you ever found
a feather?

Birds are the only animals
that have feathers.

Feathers keep birds warm.

Feathers help birds fly.

Look at this parrot fly!

Wings help birds fly, too.

All birds have wings, but not all birds fly.

Ostriches have wings, but they do not fly. Ostriches run.

Penguins have wings, too. They do not fly. They swim.

penguins

Birds have backbones.

The backbone supports the bird's body.

Animals with backbones are **vertebrates**.

Parrots have backbones.

That means parrots are vertebrates.

This parrot is with its babies.

Birds have beaks.

They use their beaks to eat fish, nuts, insects, and other kinds of food.

This bird is a kingfisher.

It uses its beak to catch fish.

beak

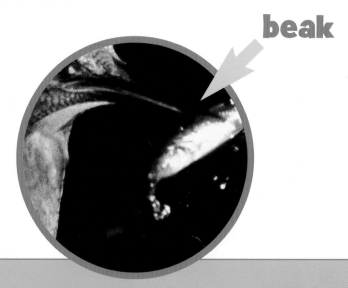

Birds are warm-blooded.

Warm-blooded means
the body temperature
stays the same.

Penguins live in
cold places.

The air outside is cold, but
their bodies stay warm.

PARTS OF A BIRD

Here is an X-ray of a swallow.

wing ——————→

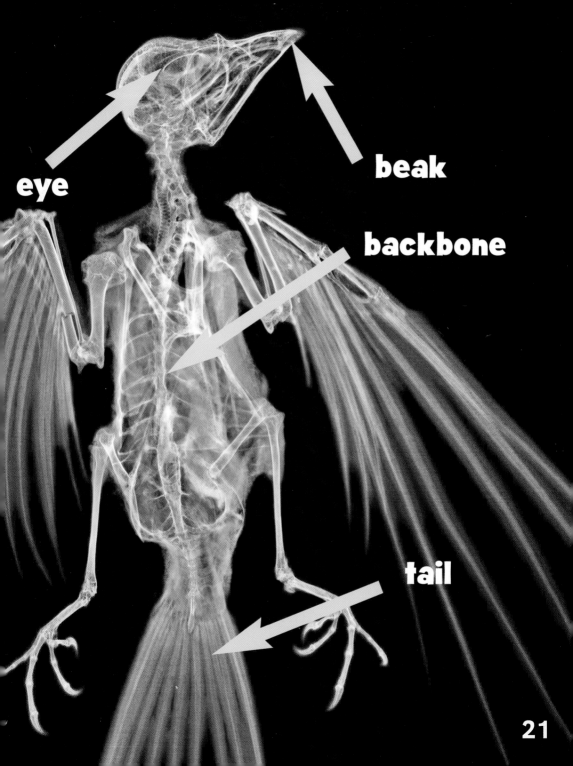

eye

beak

backbone

tail

21

YOUR NEW WORDS

clutch (kluhch) a group of eggs

feathers (**feth**-urs) light coverings on a bird's body

ostrich (**oss**-trich) a large bird in Africa that can run fast but cannot fly

parrot (**pa**-ruht) a bird that has a hooked beak and has brightly colored feathers

penguins (**peng**-gwinz) water birds that swim; They do not fly

vertebrate (**vur**-tuh-brate) an animal that has a backbone

wing (wing) a feather-covered part of a bird's body that helps it fly

ARE THESE BIRDS?

REMEMBER, BIRDS HAVE FEATHERS AND BEAKS.

bat

butterfly

dragonfly

flying squirrel

INDEX

FIND OUT MORE
Book:
Birds: A True Book, by Melissa Stewart (Children's Press, 2001)

Website:
http://www.enchantedlearning.com/subjects/birds/

MEET THE AUTHOR:
Mary Schulte is a newspaper photo editor and author of books and articles for children. She is the author of the other animal classification books in this series. She lives in Kansas City, Missouri, where her favorite bird to watch is the cardinal.